GOLDFISH CA
FOR BEGINNERS

ULTIMATE BEGINNERS GUIDE ON
HOW TO CARE FOR YOUR GOLDFISH
AND EVERYTHING YOU NEED TO
KNOW TO KEEP THEM WELL

CHARLES PENNYFEATHER

Table of Contents

Introduction 4

Chapter One 7

Where the Goldfish Pet Came From 7

Natural Goldfish Habitat 9

Are Goldfish Long-Lived Animals? 9

Are Goldfish Easy to Care For? 9

Chapter Two 11

Care for goldfish 11

Setup for a goldfish tank 12

Reasons to avoid keeping goldfish in bowls. 12

Size of a Goldfish Tank 12

The temperature of the goldfish tank 13

Filtration and Water Quality 14

Decorations for fish tanks 16

Chapter Three 19

What Do Goldfish Eat? 19

2

Behaviour and Compatibility of Goldfish 21

Typical Appearance and Behavior 22

Are Goldfish Good With Other Fish? 22

Detecting and Addressing Disease Issues 25

Goldfish Health Indicators 27

Signs of a healthy animal 27

A Red Flag (If you see any of these symptoms, call your vet.) 28

Typical Health Problems 29

FAQs 31

Introduction

The most common aquarium fish and pet fish are goldfish.

This fish is available in various hues, forms, and dimensions at all pet stores. You may inexpensively have a charming pet that you can enjoy for many years thanks to widespread breeding.

Goldfish can be taken care of properly by anybody who is persistent enough. Once you've set up the basics, they're simple to administer. However, one thing to remember about them is that because of their frigid temperatures, it may be pretty challenging to locate pals for them to live with.

They are often quiet and unobtrusive. Once your tank is set up, all that's left to do is routinely maintain its cleanliness. This entails monthly water replacement for half the tank.

Sadly, gastrointestinal problems may still affect goldfish, even on an essential diet. They can eat all day long so you won't have an issue with their hunger. This implies that goldfish create a significant quantity of waste daily and that most of their ailments are often intestinal.

Several species of goldfish are covered in this book, including:
- Faintail
- Oranda
- Black Moor
- Ryukin
- Pearlscale
- Wakin
- Ranchu
- Tosakin
- Bubble eye
- Shubunkin
- Comet

Now that you have a general understanding of the goldfish, continue reading to learn more about this fantastic fish!

Chapter One

Where the Goldfish Pet Came From

China was the first country to recognize the goldfish's potential as a domestic pet. During the Tang Dynasty (6th century A.D.), mankind domesticated the carp. Then it started the artificial selection process by breeding several carp species to produce fish with a golden colour.

Another common misconception is that koi are just more giant goldfish. They belong to two distinct species! Avoid confusing the smaller goldfish with its larger relative, the koi fish, a different carp species.

Goldfish breeding for cosmetic reasons had become so familiar by the ninth century A.D. Only royalty may own the yellow-coloured fish. On the other hand, the simple people preserved the orange ones. Although they were mainly kept outside in ponds for exhibition, they were eventually introduced into the home, progressively changing how long they would live. After some time, they were transported to Japan in the early 1600s before being sent on to other European nations.

The goldfish was a well-liked luck and fortune emblem throughout Europe. To commemorate their first wedding anniversary, married men presented their spouse's goldfish as a sign of the prosperous years to come in their union. The custom was abandoned as goldfish became more widely available since anybody could purchase something that had previously been so uncommon.
The goldfish was ultimately brought to America by the middle of the 1800s; the rest is history.

Natural Goldfish Habitat

Typically, goldfish live in watery habitats.

They thrive in a body of water that is slightly viscous, much as their carp progenitor did. They prefer slow water, no matter the temperature or environment.

Are Goldfish Long-Lived Animals?

Even though a goldfish may live for up to 15 years with adequate care if it's unlucky enough to make it that long, you'll have to flush it down the toilet in less than three years.

Your goldfish may be able to enjoy its best live up to old age with the perfect tank size, conditions, nutrition, and timely feeding!

Are Goldfish Easy to Care For?

A goldfish requires very little maintenance, and that is an understatement. If you're purchasing a goldfish for the first time, like with any other pet, you can't simply decide on a whim.

You'll undoubtedly get your money's worth if you grasp how to care for a goldfish straightforwardly and plainly.

Consider where to put it and the equipment you will need along the road. However, you must maintain it in a tank since goldfish ultimately outgrow bowls.

Next, learn about the animal's nutrition and establish a feeding regimen. The upkeep of its tank, which is essential for its existence, should also be planned.

Chapter Two
Care for goldfish

To keep your goldfish healthy, it's necessary to maintain excellent water quality with frequent water changes and proper filtration.

Check the filter, the water temperature, and other equipment daily.

At least once every week, test the quality of the water.

Every two to four weeks, or as necessary, replace 10 to 25% of the water—monthly filter media replacement.

Avoid crowded areas since they are a significant source of stress and sickness.

Setup for a goldfish tank

Your pet goldfish's development will be influenced by the tank and configuration you choose.

Whether you want to keep your pet goldfish happy or add more fish, you must be ready for proper tank upkeep. Let's look at some crucial things below and then continue our discussion on how to do this:

Reasons to avoid keeping goldfish in bowls.

Although keeping a pet goldfish in a bowl is clichéd, it won't live very long.

Even a fancy goldfish kind, which is smaller, would find swimming in such a tight place to be quite stressful. Your pet's immune system might be impacted by a stressful atmosphere, which can turn it into a sick fish.

Size of a Goldfish Tank

You should keep your pet goldfish in a giant tank you can afford; it is strongly advised. The volume of water in a larger tank may aid in temperature control.

Getting at least a 10-gallon tank for one goldfish and a 20-gallon tank for two goldfish is a decent rule of thumb for the goldfish tank size.

Soon, you could get interested in other fish species. It will be an excellent chance to introduce more fish or several kinds of goldfish! Who knows, though?

Last but not least, a decent tank size may be crucial, but oxygen absorption must also be considered. In addition to the fact that goldfish need a lot of oxygen, they also defecate, which, if left unattended, may poison the water.

The temperature of the goldfish tank

Although the water quality in your goldfish tank should be your primary concern, the temperature is also crucial for goldfish health.

The level of comfort in the water must be sufficient for your goldfish. You will need a heater to assist in controlling and maintaining a consistent temperature.

So what is the ideal temperature you should keep in your goldfish tank? An excellent range would be between 68 and 74 degrees Fahrenheit.

This is particularly relevant to fancy goldfish, whose bodies are less able to withstand colder temperatures than their ordinary goldfish counterparts. They do well in water that is warmer than 72°F. However, common goldfish can survive in water as cold as 64 degrees Fahrenheit.

Filtration and Water Quality

You may have seen a few goldfish housed in bowls at your neighbourhood pet shop that appeared to be doing well.

But don't be deceived. In addition to having little to no swimming room, these bowls' low water quality will harm your new fish's health. The filtration system is thus a crucial component of having a goldfish aquarium or goldfish tank.

Due to their voracious appetites and prodigious feces, your pet goldfish will unavoidably pollute its surroundings and consume excessive food. Water has to be changed often to stop this from occurring.

So how can a decent filtration system help you care for your goldfish?

In essence, you need the water to continue flowing continuously. A robust filtering system guards your goldfish against being poisoned and inactivity, which builds up an excess of food and nutrients.

To breathe effectively underwater, goldfish need a lot of oxygen; thus, efficient filtration is necessary to promote air circulation and draw air from the surface into the water.

Finally, it aids in the purification of tainted water, which is one of the primary reasons for goldfish disease.

You are strongly advised to choose an external filter that hangs next to your goldfish tank. Even though it is more expensive, it is ten times more effective than the internal one. It won't take up any tank capacity.

Decorations for fish tanks

The next stage of our goldfish care trip will be more fun: goldfish tank decorations!

Aquarium fish often circle a little underwater castle in the media. Of course, you have to consider the size of your goldfish tank and ensure there is adequate swimming room for your goldfish before going to the pet shop and purchasing anything like that. The substance must also be non-toxic to prevent lowering water quality.

What precisely is the first step, then?
Goldfish may live without a substrate, but having one can increase the surface area necessary for healthy bacteria's growth. The substrate must first be selected since it differs for each species. For instance, pea gravel endangers goldfish. This helpful bacterium aids in preserving nitrogen levels, which are essential to the general health of goldfish.

Plants are the next. But are they essential? Do you purchase a phony one or a real one? Because they are known to eat everything, goldfish are known to destroy aquatic vegetation.

Because of this, it's essential only to purchase live plants suitable for an aquarium with goldfish. A robust plant, for instance, can withstand being decimated by a goldfish.

On the other hand, because fake ones do an excellent job of making goldfish tanks appear appealing regardless, some goldfish owners choose to decorate with them. They seem much simpler to maintain and more vivid than genuine ones.

The advantages of growing live plants, however, still outweigh the drawbacks. They enhance water quality by absorbing CO_2 emissions and exhaling oxygen into the tank, which helps maintain an appropriate amount of oxygen.

Last but not least, be careful to do the decor sparingly. Corals, wood, pebbles, and plastics should not be used. These items often include components that might improve or harm the system in your goldfish tank.

Corals sometimes even contain parasites that may infect your fish. Toxic substances may also be found in other things, so be careful what you put inside.

Chapter Three

What Do Goldfish Eat?

Keep in mind that goldfish are omnivores and will essentially consume any food. How can you balance their food to provide a healthy goldfish diet?

They should primarily be fed a combination of specialty goldfish flakes and pellets, with freeze-dried brine shrimp and a few finely chopped vegetables as preferred additions. Additionally, it's a good idea to provide a few tubifex worms as a reward.

Goldfish are often advised to eat twice or three times daily to maintain a balanced diet or, at the very least, control their constant appetites. However, novices unfamiliar with goldfish care tend to overfeed these gentle fish.

Ensure that your goldfish can consume each piece you offer in under two minutes. Anything more than that would add to the pollution in their tank, which would eventually be harmful to them.

Behaviour and Compatibility of Goldfish

Since goldfish are generally calm fish, maintaining them is pretty simple. They can distinguish their owner from others, believe it or not. Do you now feel unique?

Goldfish, meanwhile, like socializing with other fish. However, since a goldfish prefers a colder environment, other fish must also be able to withstand its temperature requirements. Make sure the fish in your aquarium has a comparable size and temperament before introducing them.

Although goldfish are gregarious, lively, and clever, finding their tank mates can sometimes be challenging.

Typical Appearance and Behavior

- Compared to other fish, their size, regular presence, and conduct produce more waste and need powerful filtration.
- Multicoloured goldfish's colour patterns might vary over time.
- Slower swimmers that enjoy calm, slow-moving water.
- They are a gregarious species that may eventually learn to identify their pet parent.
- Over time, they could take food from your palm with ease.

Are Goldfish Good With Other Fish?

The selection of the ideal goldfish partners is the most challenging phase in building a successful business with these freshwater fish. Goldfish are unique compared to most tropical fish sold in commerce. There are several qualities to take into account while choosing possible tank mates.

Avoid the temptation to overstock the aquarium with fish. Ammonia levels will rise due to congestion, water oxygen levels will drop, and your fish will perish. It would be best to consider the habitat other fish need to live in.

The new fish you add to your goldfish aquarium must tolerate the same temperature and nutrition as your goldfish.

Goldfish that are safely housed alone need a lot of swimming room. Fancy goldfish cannot be kept alongside regular goldfish, comets, or shubunkins.

While ranchus get along with other fancy sorts like orandas, black moors, and fantails.

Speed plays a significant role since quicker fish may devour all the food before the finer fish can finish their allotment. On the other side, fancier goldfish are slower and more likely to nip, which may be why.

In addition, goldfish tend to eat smaller fish as they become more prominent. The smaller fish, which they won't see as prey since they are used to their presence, and with whom they grew up, make this very improbable, according to sources. The possibility that they may consume their more petite buddy is likewise uncertain.

Detecting and Addressing Disease Issues

Goldfish are susceptible to sickness despite their toughness if not given the correct care.

It's possible that a sick goldfish came from less-than-ideal circumstances. Additionally, you must have exposed them when introducing a new fish without isolating them.

Sometimes, a few days after you bring them home from the pet shop, they might get an ailment out of the blue. Most likely, they had carried something with them from the beginning.

This type of problem is common in goldfish husbandry. It will often put you to the test, but the learning is invaluable, so overall it's a win-win situation.

The symptoms of goldfish water poisoning are similar to those of other disorders. It will be easier to assess your fish's prognosis if you can identify the problem as soon as feasible. The condition of your fish will have a better chance of improving if you can identify the issue earlier.

Goldfish with illnesses often live in unsanitary tanks. It is crucial to check the water because this is constant. Although it can seem clean initially, it is poisonous and will make your skin itch. Since goldfish are known to create a lot of waste, this is particularly true when you often forget to replace the water. Eventually, the water will become poisoned.

Ammonia and nitrite can only be two of the causes of the fish's illness. There may be a lot of harmful side effects, even a tiny amount.

If you maintain your poor goldfish in a filthy environment, parasites, bacterial illnesses, and fungal diseases will wreak havoc. Your fish will be eaten until they cannot defend their life if you don't take prompt action and let these spread.

The good news is that your goldfish will still have the chance to grow and be happy for many years to come if you can identify such ailments early on.

But pay attention! Never provide any medicine without thoroughly comprehending the underlying cause of the illness. Make sure you've done your homework and sought advice from professionals.

Goldfish Health Indicators

Signs of a healthy animal

- Lucid Eyes
- Optimum Appetite

- Healthy Breathing
- Parasite- and Disease-free

A Red Flag (If you see any of these symptoms, call your vet.)

- Reduced Appetite
- Absence of colour
- Blemishes or fungus in the mouth or body
- Labored Breathing
- Listlessness
- Pop-eye or cloudy vision increases the scales
- Fins with tears or discoloration
- Inconsistency or difficulty swimming
- Loss of weight
- Bloating

Typical Health Problems

Health Issues	Symptoms or Causes	Action Recommendation
Ich	The body and fins of the fish develop white patches, and it scrapes against hard surfaces or swims erratically. rapid breathing	Put fish into quarantine immediately, apply commercial ich remedies as indicated, and add freshwater aquarium salt. Consult a local aquatic veterinarian or expert.
Bacterial infections	Cloudy eyes, open sores and/or	Improve water quality; add aquarium salt; use a commercial antibacterial remedy as directed; consult your local aquatic specialist or

	reddening of the skin.	aquatic veterinarian for treatment
Fungus	White cottony growth and/or discoloration of the eyes.	Quarantine fish; use a commercial antifungal remedy as directed. Consult your local aquatic specialist or aquatic veterinarian.
Fin rot	Frayed or disintegrating fins; the base of the fins usually reddens.	Improve water quality; consult your local aquatic specialist or aquatic veterinarian for treatment.

FAQs

Question	Answer
Do goldfish live a long time?	With adequate care, goldfish may live up to 15 years on average and up to 30 years in certain species.
How big can goldfish get?	A comet goldfish may grow 18 inches long as an adult.
What are the goldfish fed?	Due to their omnivorous nature, goldfish should be fed a range of flakes, pellets, freeze-dried, and frozen meals.

Which tank size should I get for a goldfish?	Since goldfish create more waste than other fish species, it's ideal to provide a young goldfish with at least a 20-gallon aquarium.
How should a goldfish be cared for?	Goldfish should be kept in a properly constructed, cleaned, and decorated aquarium. Every day, they need to be offered a balanced meal.
What kind of fish may coexist with goldfish?	Since goldfish are a cold-water species, it is ideal for keeping them in a tank alongside other

	cold-water fish like white cloud minnows.
When do you feed your goldfish?	Goldfish should only be given food they can finish in one to two minutes once a day in small amounts.
From where do goldfish originate?	East Asia is home to native goldfish.
How much time can goldfish spend without eating?	Goldfish may go up to two weeks without eating. But just as much as they can take in 1 to 2 minutes should be provided to them once a day to maintain their best health.
What do the eggs of goldfish look like?	Goldfish eggs may be white or yellow and

	resemble tiny, transparent bubbles.
How many goldfish can you fit in a gallon-sized aquarium at once?	As a rough guideline, 5 gallons are needed for every inch of an adult goldfish's length.
Do betta fish and goldfish get along?	Because goldfish and bettas need separate habitats, avoiding housing them in the same tank is preferable.
Can goldfish survive in a bowl?	Goldfish may grow to adult sizes of 5 to 18 inches, depending on the species chosen. They should be kept in an aquarium of at least 20 gallons (for juveniles).

| What can you feed goldfish? | Due to their omnivorous nature, goldfish should be fed a range of flakes, pellets, freeze-dried, and frozen meals. |

Printed in Great Britain
by Amazon